MY VERY FIRST

Word Book

ANGELA WILKES

DORLING KINDERSLEY

LONDON • NEW YORK • STUTTGART

DK

A DORLING KINDERSLEY BOOK

First published in Great Britain in 1993
by Dorling Kindersley Limited,
9 Henrietta Street, London WC2E 8PS
Reprinted 1994
Copyright © 1993 Dorling Kindersley Limited, London

Photography (p.21 frog) copyright © 1990 Jerry Young
Photography (back cover & p.21 rabbit)
copyright © 1991 Barrie Watts

A CIP catalogue record for this book is
available from the British Library

ISBN 0-7513-5099-0

Colour reproduction by Colourscan
Printed in Italy by L.E.G.O.

Contents

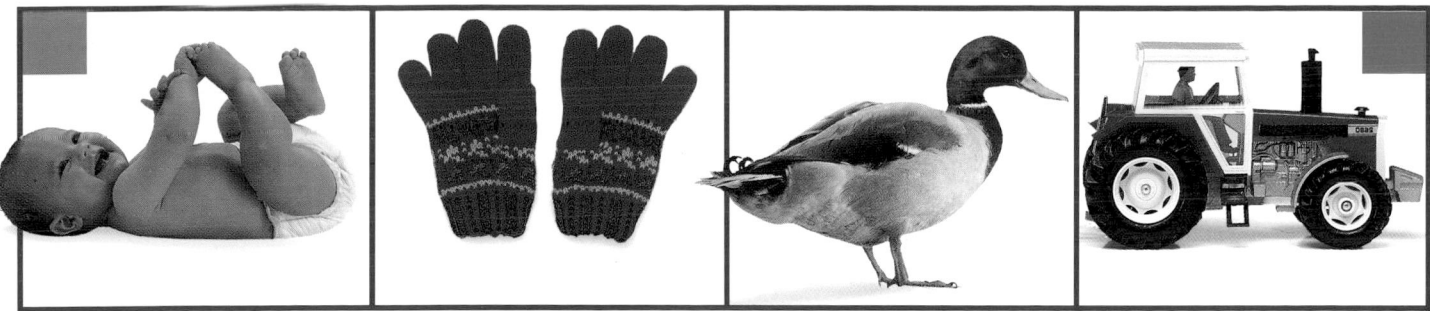

Note to parents and teachers

My Very First Word Book is a bright and colourful catalogue of words and pictures for you and your child to share. Packed with photographs of everyday objects, it is the ideal way to introduce young children to written words.

Children will enjoy recognizing and naming familiar objects. You can encourage your child to associate each image with the written word by pointing to the picture as you read out the word label. This is one of the very first steps in learning to read.

The book is organized in themes, beginning with a child's immediate experience of home and daily activities, and extending to a wider range of topics, such as animals and machines. By reading the pages in order, children will gradually increase their spoken vocabulary. An alphabetical index has been included so that children can use the book as a first picture dictionary.

With so many pictures to look at and talk about, this book offers a variety of other learning opportunities. You can talk about shapes, sizes, colours, and patterns, and encourage your child to count, compare, and sort the objects on every page.

All about me

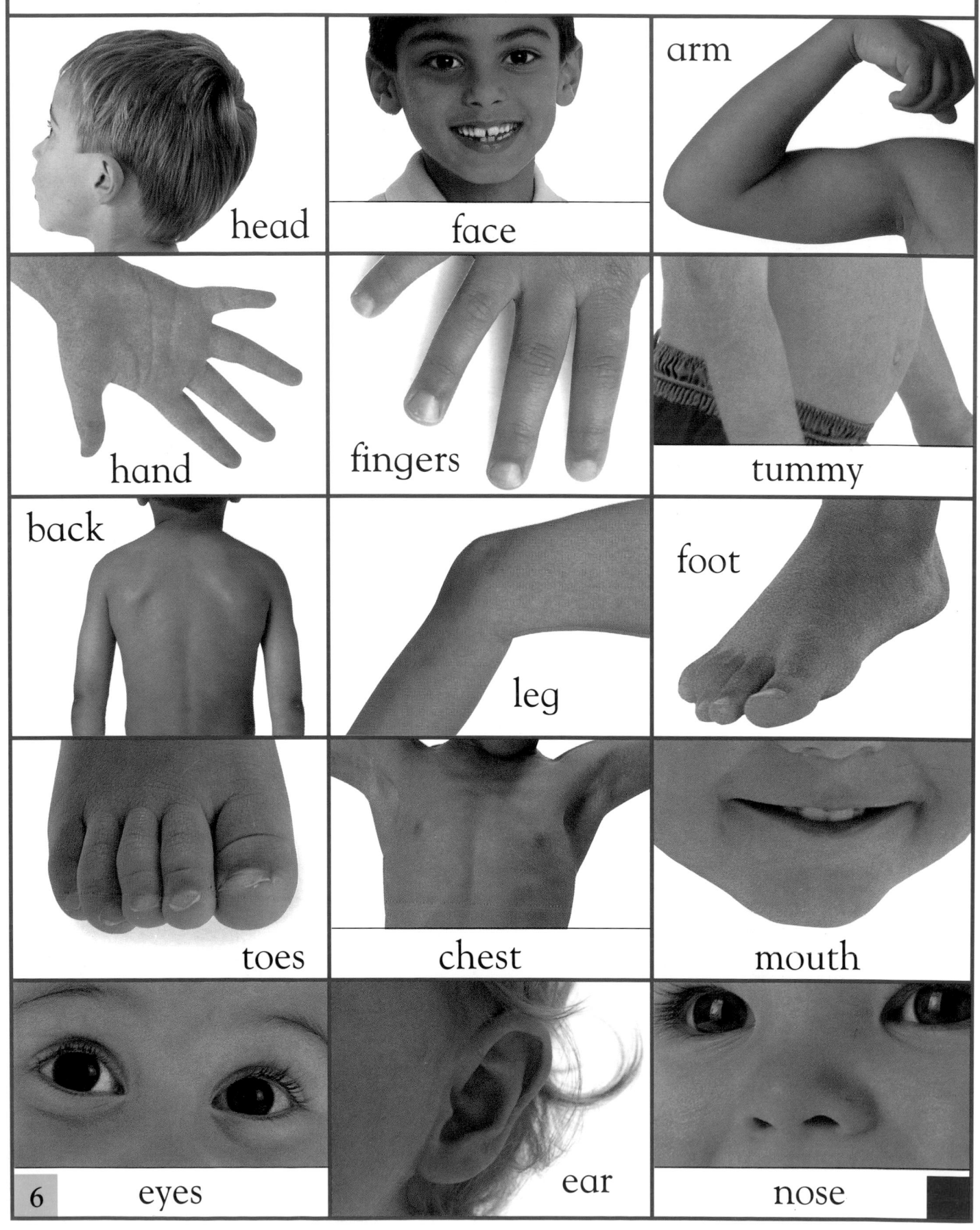

head

face

arm

hand

fingers

tummy

back

leg

foot

toes

chest

mouth

eyes

ear

nose

6

Getting dressed

vest

pants

trousers

socks

dress

skirt

T-shirt

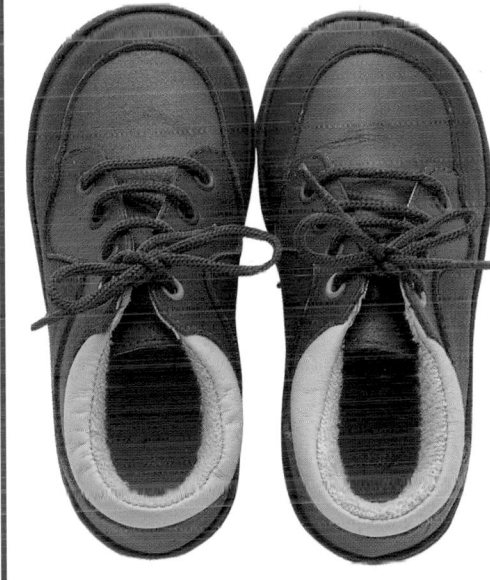

shoes

tights

jumper

7

Mealtime

chair

table

egg

bowl

plate

yoghurt

spoon

mug

apple

knife   fork

8

orange

pasta

grapes

tomatoes

biscuits

bread

cheese

raisins

juice

milk

banana

9

At home

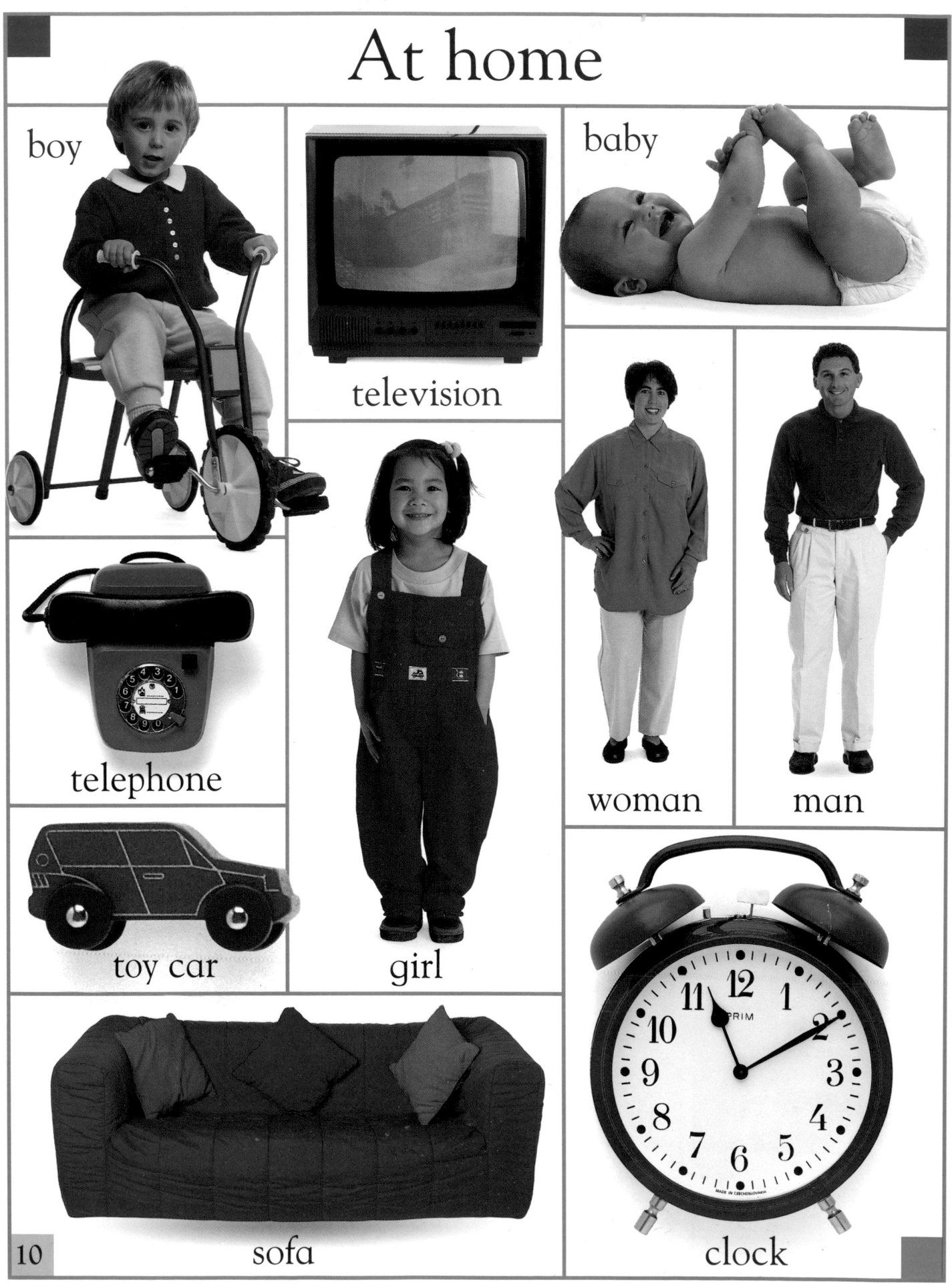

boy

television

baby

telephone

woman

man

toy car

girl

10 sofa

clock

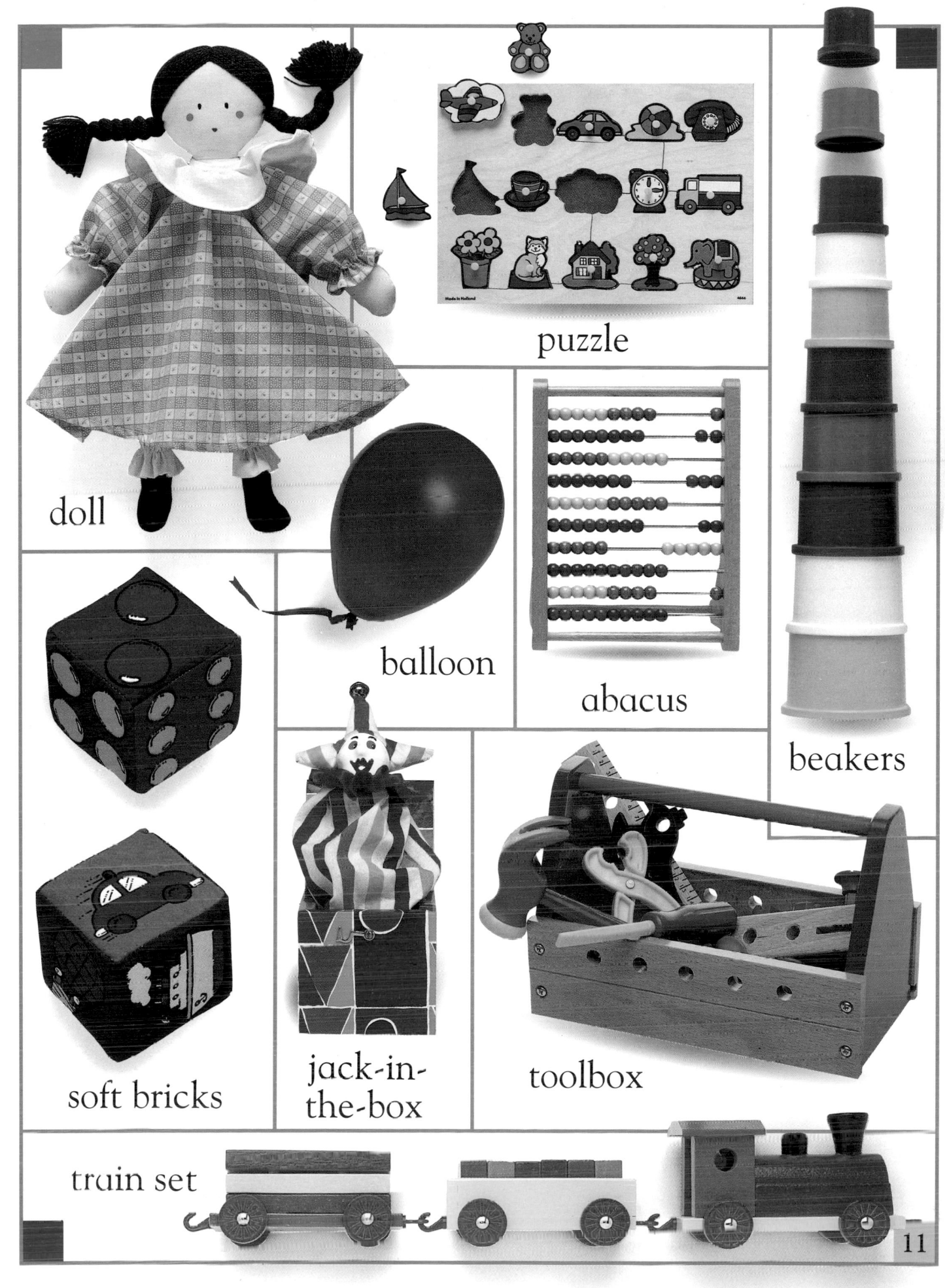

doll

puzzle

balloon

abacus

beakers

soft bricks

jack-in-
the-box

toolbox

train set

11

Going out

coat

gloves

woolly hat

scarf

ball

bucket

spade

12 boots

buggy

umbrella

bicycle

tree

leaves

duck

bird

slide

seesaw

kite

Bedtime

sponge

brush

comb

potty

taps

towel

shampoo

soaps

bath

toothpaste

toothbrush

14

mobile

bed

lamp

teddy bear

dressing gown

pyjamas

cot

slippers

blanket

Things that go

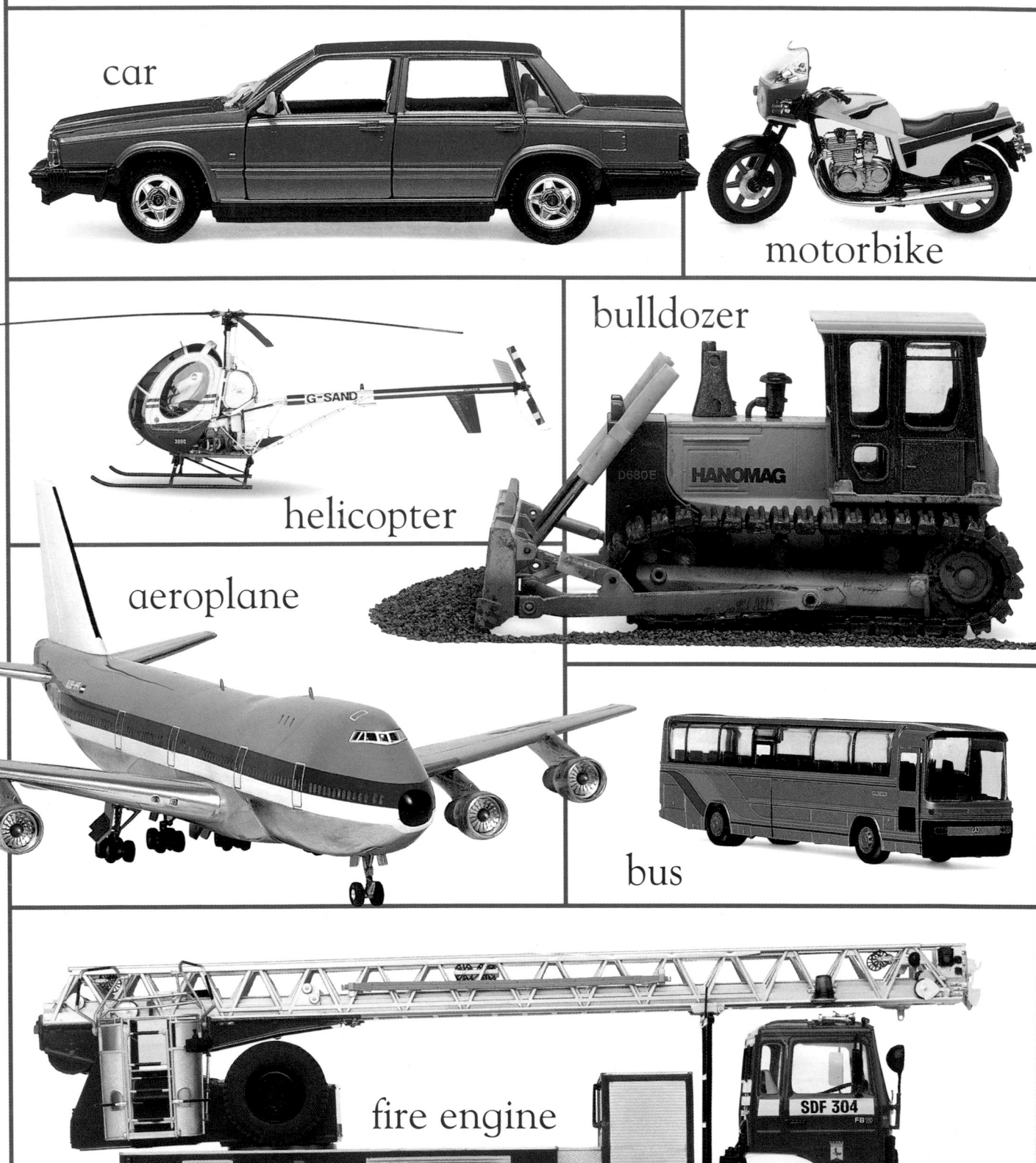

car

motorbike

helicopter

bulldozer

aeroplane

bus

fire engine

SDF 304

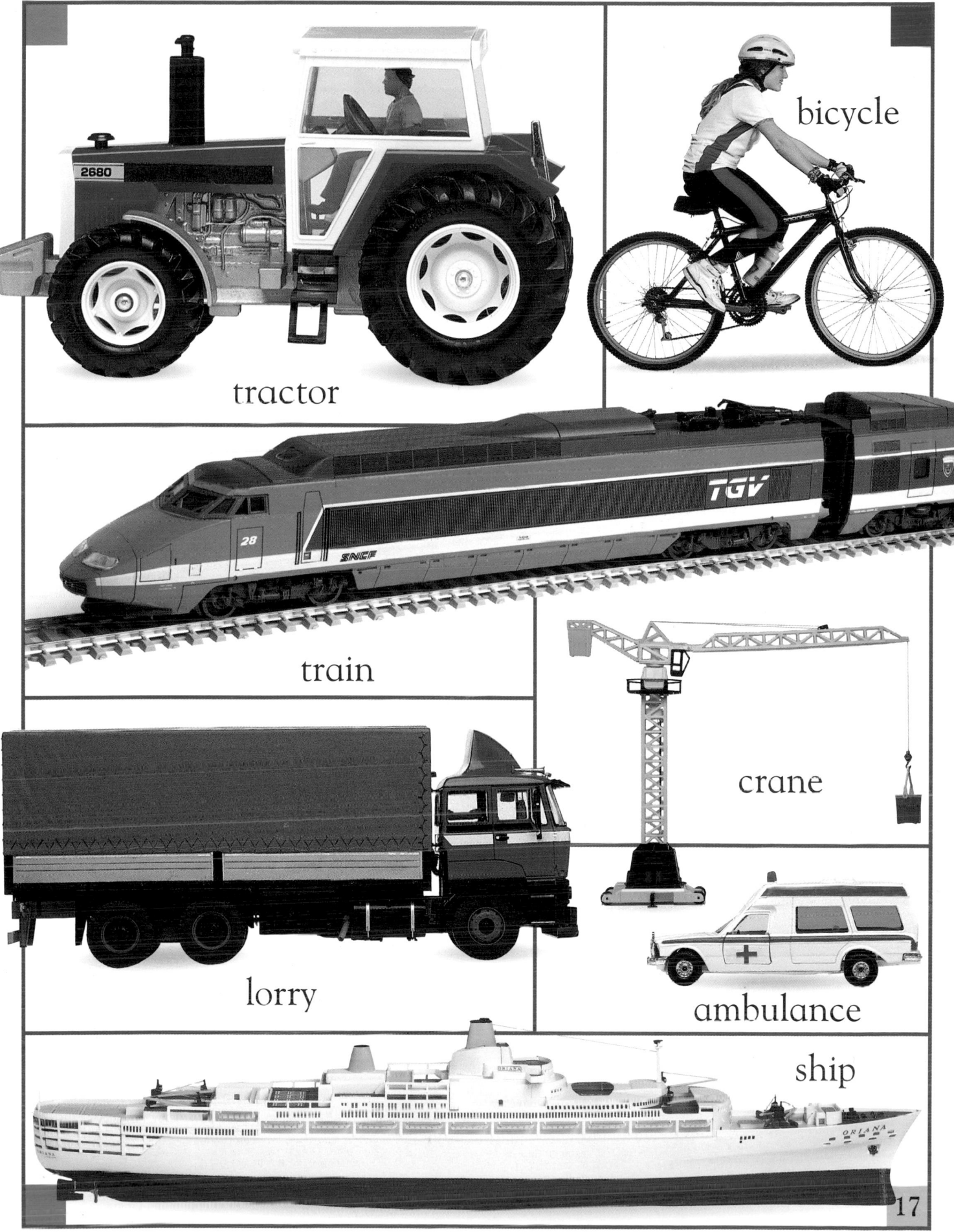

tractor

bicycle

train

lorry

crane

ambulance

ship

Animals

kittens

puppies

cat

dog

goldfish

horse

cow

calf

hen

mouse

chicks

pig

cockerel

rabbit

sheep

lamb

goose

budgerigars

Counting

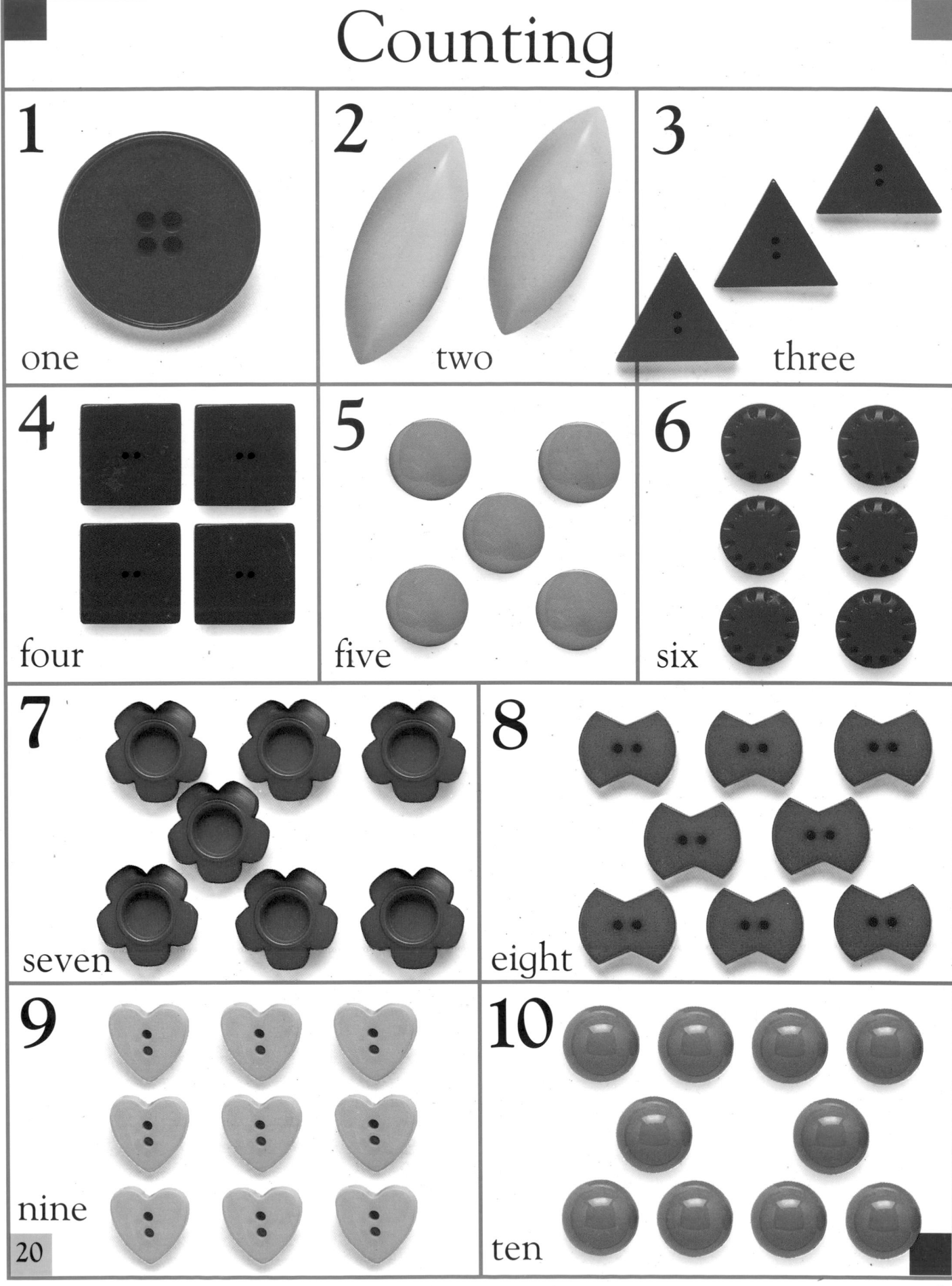

1 one

2 two

3 three

4 four

5 five

6 six

7 seven

8 eight

9 nine

10 ten

Colours

red

blue

yellow

green

pink

purple

orange

black

white

brown

silver

gold

Index